Original title:
All Shades of Christmas

Copyright © 2024 Creative Arts Management OÜ
All rights reserved.

Author: Elliot Harrison
ISBN HARDBACK: 978-9916-90-838-9
ISBN PAPERBACK: 978-9916-90-839-6

**The Spirit of Old and New**

Eggnog drinks and fruitcake fright,
Uncle Bob's socks, a terrible sight.
Kids hide from Santa's snow-white beard,
While belly laughs drown out their weird.

Old tales told by the crackling fire,
Grandma's dance moves spark wild desire.
Vintage ornaments shine bright as stars,
Remind us of past jingle-jangle jars.

## Melodies of Mirth at Dusk

Singing off-key beneath the tree,
A cat meows in perfect harmony.
Chorus echoing through the night,
While cookies vanish, out of sight.

Pine cones rolling down the hill,
Laughter erupts, it's quite the thrill.
Neighbors peeking through the frosted glass,
Cheering on as we all dance en masse.

## **A Tangle of Joyful Lights**

Twinkling bulbs on the porch look great,
Until the raccoons think it's their plate.
Tangled wires and a ladder's tilt,
A spectacle made of colorful guilt.

Chasing shadows under the moon,
Tripping over the dog—what a cartoon!
Sparkling garlands and silly hats,
Creating chaos, oh, where's the cat?

## **Petals of Warmth in Cold**

Poinsettias bloom, yet somehow sneeze,
Every hug feels like a warm breeze.
A knitted scarf, two sizes too big,
Wrapped around dad—what a funny fig!

Roasting chestnuts in a dandy pan,
But flares up smoke instead of a plan.
Gifts in wrappers, lopsided and bright,
Wait till the dog finds them tonight!

**Dappled Lights in Winter's Embrace**

Twinkling bulbs on the tree,
Cats think it's their new toy.
Tinsel stuck to my hair,
My aunt's laugh brings such joy.

Snowflakes dance in the breeze,
Hot cocoa spills on my shirt.
Wrapping gifts with great ease,
Then watch as my dog goes berserk.

## **Chromatic Carols in the Air**

Singing songs off the key,
The choir's not quite in tune.
Grandma's cookies all miss,
Guess it's burnt within a swoon.

Reindeer games in the yard,
Uncle Joe's a little spry.
Who knew snowballs could fly,
While dodging the neighbor's cat?

## Shades of Togetherness and Love

Family gathered 'round,
Mismatched sweaters on display.
Nanny's stories abound,
I hope they won't last all day.

Auntie's dance moves are bold,
Flipping cookies on the floor.
She claims they're pure gold,
But they're really a food war.

**Starlit Nights and Joyful Blights**

Under lights that are bright,
We chase shadows on the wall.
The ornaments take flight,
And my brother takes a fall.

Elves in the shopping spree,
Buying gifts with wild glee.
Amidst all the chaos seen,
Laughter's the best kind of spree.

## **The Color of Comfort**

Red nose on a reindeer, oh what a sight,
Santa sipping cocoa, such pure delight.
Cookies on the table, crumbs everywhere,
Elves on the shelves, they giggle and stare.

Snowmen in the front yard, hats askew,
Frosty's stuck in a dance, who knew?
Stockings stuffed with treats, candy galore,
Grandma's secret fruitcake, never ask for more.

## A Symphony of Seasonal Delights

Carolers in the street, off-key but loud,
Mistletoe mishaps, under it we crowd.
Fluttering snowflakes, a whimsical show,
Winter's just a grin, don't you love the glow?

Yule logs are crackling, sparks flying high,
Socks on the floor, oh me, oh my!
Gravy spills and laughter, a joyful mess,
Pass the mashed potatoes, I must confess.

## **Garlands of Gratitude**

Twinkling lights tangled, what a surprise,
Grandpa lost in the tree, oh how he tries.
Thankfulness woven in ribbons so bright,
Uncle Joe's bad jokes bring pure delight.

Cards filled with wishes, some a bit vague,
Rabbits in the garden, the oddest plague.
Laughter fills the room, the best kind of cheer,
As we toast to the year, I'll bring the beer.

## Laughter in the Lantern Glow

Lanterns are glowing, casting soft light,
Kids sneak in snacks, a true Christmas sight.
Bells on the door jingle with cheer,
Stray cats in costumes, oh dear, oh dear.

Hot cocoa spills, the dog runs away,
Chasing his tail, brightening the day.
Sledding and laughter, falling with style,
Snowballs are flying, let's play for a while.

## A Quilt of Community and Kindness

Neighbors hang lights, all tangled tight,
Cats chase ribbons, oh what a sight!
Cookies baked, and burnt too late,
We laugh and sigh, it's all first rate.

Chili spills, a dog jumps high,
Kids with snowballs ready to fly.
Mismatched socks, and hats askew,
Together we shine, just like the dew.

## The Beauty of Togetherness

Frogs in sweaters dance by the fire,
Hot cocoa spills, oh what a choir!
Grandma knits a hat for the cat,
Puppies nibble on a big Santa hat.

We're all a little nutty, that's for sure,
But the joy we share is the perfect cure.
Wrap each other up in mismatched cheer,
Raise a glass to friendship, and don't shed a tear!

## **Rustic Charm and Modern Wonders**


Trees adorned with gadgets quite bizarre,
Cider mixed with a splash of stir bar.
Old lanterns flicker, and glow so bright,
While selfies flash, capturing the night.

Nutcrackers dance, with a twist and a spin,
And Auntie's jokes make my cheeks turn crimson.
Embracing the chaos, we twirl and we tease,
With laughter and love, we're always at ease.

## The Alchemy of Celebration

Balloons that pop, and confetti rain,
A turkey trip, oh what a strain!
Jingle bells echo with goofy glee,
As we all trip over the fallen tree.

Magic in moments, a toast with cheer,
Laughter that echoes, spreading good cheer.
Life's bubbling over, like soda gone wild,
In the joy of each gathering, we're all reconciled.

## **Hues of Hope and Joy**

The reindeer dance in tangled lights,
While Santa's stuck in chimney sights.
Elves are laughing, making toys,
Who knew they'd be such noisy boys?

Mistletoe hangs, a sticky trap,
Kisses claimed by Grandma's lap.
Hot cocoa spills, marshmallows roam,
Sipping joy at our festive home.

## Beneath the Winter Sky

Snowmen argue about their hats,
Frosty found he's got no stats.
Warming hands on cookies hot,
Who ate them all? We have no shot!

Sledding down the hill so fast,
With laughter that we hope will last.
Bumps and flips, a tumble here,
We end up giggling - oh dear, oh dear!

## A Tapestry of Tidings

Gifts unraveled with a cheer,
One's a sweater that won't fit near.
Grandpa's snoring on the couch,
While cats are scheming to pouch!

Bright lights twinkle, a sight to see,
Neighbors compete—who's best? It's me!
Pine needles scattered, a slippery fate,
Watch your step or you'll just wait!

## Shadows of Celebration

Carols sung with off-key flair,
Dogs join in, but don't seem to care.
Gingerbread dreams get crushed like pie,
Iced on the floor, oh my, oh my!

Chasing cookies, seeking the last,
Time flies quick, this season's a blast.
As laughter echoes, joy's the prize,
Each silly moment, the best of our lives.

## **Soft Glows and Bright Hopes**

Twinkling lights on a tree, oh what a sight,
A squirrel steals a bauble, what a funny plight.
Cats in Santa hats, prancing with glee,
The dog looks confused, where's his cup of tea?

Eggnog spills on my shoes, what a clumsy dance,
A reindeer on the roof, does it ever prance?
Snowmen in the yard, with a floppy old hat,
They all seem to giggle, how silly is that!

## The Fire's Embrace and the Chill Outside

The fireplace crackles, as marshmallows toast,
Dad claims he's a chef, but we all know the most.
Mom juggles her cookies, a sight to behold,
While brother's in the corner, trying not to fold.

Outside it's a winter wonder, snowflakes that gleam,
But inside's a battle of who'll win the cream.
A snowball fight turns into a slip and slide,
In this frosty fun, we all take great pride!

## **Warmth of Togetherness**

Gathered 'round the table, food spills and flies,
Uncle tells the same joke—oh what a surprise!
Auntie spills her drink, laughter fills the air,
While the cat steals a nap, without a single care.

Homemade sweaters, itchy and bright,
A fashion disaster, but oh what delight!
Grandpa's snoring softly, the dog on his knee,
Both dreaming of feasts in sweet harmony.

## Crafting Joy from Simple Things

With glue and some sparkles, we craft with glee,
Creating odd ornaments, it's quite a spree.
Silly hats and reindeer games make us bright,
Decorating with laughter, oh what a sight!

A chorus of giggles while we sing off-key,
Trying to remember the words, oh woe are we!
But as the night whispers of comfort and cheer,
These moments together are what we hold dear.

## **Whispers of Winter's Glow**

In a snowy land where penguins dance,
A squirrel dressed up in a bright red pants.
The reindeer giggle, wearing silly hats,
As snowflakes twirl like playful acrobats.

The cocoa spills, oh what a sight!
Marshmallows jump with pure delight.
A snowman slips, he takes a bow,
"Who's the clumsy one? Well, that's me now!"

## Tinsel Dreams and Evergreen Hues

A tree that sparkles, one big odd sight,
With ornaments fighting to hang on tight.
The cats chase ribbons, in wild pursuit,
While Grandma's fruitcake makes everyone mute.

The lights blink on, then off they go,
Like tiny parties, all in a row.
A gingerbread house, a sticky delight,
Just don't ask the sweet tooth for a bite!

## A Palette of Holiday Spirit


The stockings hang, full of hope and cheer,
But each seems to smell like last month's beer.
The elves are busy, yet nap all day,
While Santa's on break, doing ballet!

The cookies vanish; were they ever there?
On the table? Oh no! More in the air!
A sleigh with wheels? Oh what a treat!
Will Rudolph drive? I think he'll cheat!

## Festive Lights on Frosted Nights

Icicles hang like uh-ohs from the roof,
While snowmen build a snowball proof.
The carolers sing with off-key glee,
A tune that sounds like a cat in a tree.

The holiday punch? A sugary mess,
With sprinkles that cause quite the dress distress.
But laughter rings loud, and that's the key,
In this merry, jolly, mixed-up jubilee!

**Melodies Entwined with Colorful Lights**

The lights on the tree blink in a dance,
While cat tries to pounce, oh what a chance!
Mistletoe hangs, but no one dares kiss,
They'd rather just laugh, it's too hit or miss.

The cookies are baked, yet burnt to a crisp,
Grandma's recipe called for a tiny lisp.
Singing off-key, we belt out our tunes,
Even the dog howls, he's joining our boons.

## The Rich Tapestry of Holiday Essence

Stockings are hung with care and some whim,
Filled with odd things: a shoehorn and brim.
The fruitcake's alive, it wiggles and jiggles,
Even the mouse gives it curious giggles.

With sweaters that glow and clash like a dream,
Uncles make jokes that lose all their steam.
Tangled in garlands, we laugh and we play,
While Auntie declares she's had 'just one' every day.

## **Whispers of Winter Joy**

The snowmen we built lean to one side,
They smile with carrots, yet bubbles inside.
Hot cocoa spills over, marshmallows collide,
Mom says it's fine, it's part of the ride.

We sneak to the fridge, just one cookie more,
Dad trips on the wrapping, sprawled out on the floor.
Laughter erupts as we peek through the door,
This holiday chaos, we couldn't ask for more.

## **Tinsel Dreams Unraveled**

Tinsel cascades like a shiny waterfall,
The cat's in the tree, oh dear, here we crawl.
Dad's napkin hat, he thinks it's a crown,
While the kids try to make him a royal gown.

With bows that are missing, and paper once bright,
Uncle Tim's snoring, what a comical sight.
As laughter fills rooms and plates overflow,
It's these crazy moments that brighten the glow.

## The Radiance of Unwrapped Dreams

Santa's belly jiggles, oh what a sight,
Tinsel tangles as we laugh with delight.
Kids are buzzing, cookies left out,
I hope he doesn't mind my dog running about.

Elves tied up in ribbons, they can't break free,
One's hanging upside down, giggling with glee.
The tree's a bit crooked, but we love it so,
Who needs a straight trunk when you've got that glow?

Mistletoe mishaps, a bump and a slide,
Someone slipped on the wrapping, laughter worldwide.
A reindeer in pajamas, looking quite smart,
It's the quirkiest joy that fills up the heart.

Cheeky shadows dance as the lights start to twinkle,
Bubbly joy bubbles, no chance to crinkle.
Presents are piled high, the cats start to plot,
This festive chaos is quite the jackpot!

## Flavors of the Season's Table

Cranberry sauces that wobble with grace,
Pumpkin pie faces all over the place.
Grandma's roast turkey, a sight to behold,
Yet Aunt Sue's fruitcake, well, that story is old.

Mashed potatoes fly like a fluffy white cloud,
As we gather around, all the family, loud.
Spilled grape juice stains on a tablecloth bright,
Yikes! Someone's shirt matches it just right!

Candy canes hidden in the mashed peas,
As funny little jokes make us all weak in the knees.
A dog in a sweater, oh what a thrill,
He's eyeing the table, with pure, hungry skill.

Whipped cream fights as laughter does swell,
Each bite is a giggle, you know very well.
Then comes the dance, with chairs sliding fast,
We laugh till we cry, with memories that last!

## Kisses Under the Bough

A slip and a slide, oh dear, oh my!
Kissing the air while the ball rolls by.
Mistletoe wanders, misplaced on a lamp,
Now Uncle Joe's giving Grandma a stamp!

Chatty folks under the sparkly glow,
Trying to whisper, but they're stealing the show.
Giggles erupt like soft jingle bells,
Under the branches, where chaos dwells.

Footed pajamas dance like lively sprites,
While elves in the corner are sharing their bites.
A snicker from Sam, as he dodges a kiss,
With tongues sticking out, we all scream in bliss.

More kisses, more laughter, the night's spinning fast,
Every silly moment, a joy unsurpassed.
So here's to the smiles and funny little fumbles,
With magic in air, our love never tumbles!

## Snowflakes and Sweet Surprises

Snowflakes tumble, like popcorn on the floor,
Hats flying off in a frosty uproar.
A snowman with glasses, a scarf, and a grin,
His nose is a pickle, let the laughter begin!

Sleds full of giggles, we race down the hill,
While hot cocoa spills give the dog quite a thrill.
Snowballs a-flinging, oh, duck or you'll see,
That frozen delights come wrapped up with glee!

Footprints in snow lead to sweet candy dreams,
While penguins and reindeer join in with the beams.
Surprises in stockings, what has Santa found?
A sock puppet llama, it twirls all around!

Snowflakes keep falling, a wonder they weave,
While nutcracker stitches come alive Christmas Eve.
So here's to the fun, the laughter, and cheer,
For sweet surprises await every year!

**Frosted Memories Hold Tight**

Snowflakes swirling high in the air,
Uncle Joe's toupee, caught unaware.
Mom lost her glasses, looked high and low,
Found 'em on Fido, stealing the show.

Cookies all lopsided, mix smashed on the floor,
Grandma's advice? Add chocolate—more!
The cat's wrapped in ribbons, snug as a bug,
While we sip our cider, feeling the hug.

**Echoes of Evergreen**

The tree's a bit lopsided, but that's just our flair,
Hastily hung baubles, quite the unique pair.
Tinsel's a mystery, it lands where it may,
On the dog's tail, or the gingerbread tray.

Singing off-key to our favorite tune,
Missed the last note; the dog howls at the moon.
Pine-scented chaos, laughter fills the hall,
While Dad's stuck inside the big cardboard ball.

## **Twinkling Lights and Silent Nights**

Twinkling lights twirl like a dance in the dark,
Granny's got sparks flying—who needs a park?
Mistletoe mishaps, too close to the door,
Awkward situations worth laughing for more.

Hot cocoa spills make the carpet look grand,
A marshmallow fight? Oh, that wasn't planned!
Jingle bells jingled, on the wrong tune,
As the cat takes the stage in a fuzzy costume.

**Beacons of Yuletide Spirit**

Socks hanging crooked, filled with delight,
Uncle Bob's snoring, a majestic sight.
The fire's roaring, but so is Aunt Sue,
With tales of our past and her famous stew.

Ornaments tell tales of trips to the mall,
With every weird gift, we remember it all.
The laughter rang out, like a bell in the night,
As we raise our mugs, and toast to the light.

## The Spectrum of Yuletide Joy

In reindeer suits, they prance about,
With jingle bells that never shout.
The tree's all decked in colors bright,
While cats plot mischief every night.

Gifts wrapped up like strange burritos,
With tags that say 'Hurry, eat these nachos!'
A squirrel steals the holiday snacks,
As we adjust our festive hats.

Snowmen wearing silly hats,
Spell out greetings to all the cats.
Mistletoe hung on laundry lines,
While Grandma dances to olden rhymes.

Stockings stuffed with oddities,
Like tiny toys and inner peace.
This merry chaos fills our hearts,
As laughter echoes, joy imparts.

## **Hues of Peace Beneath the Stars**

Underneath the starry sky,
A turkey tries to learn to fly.
Decorations made of gumdrops,
As carolers sing in flip-flop shops.

Santa's lost his list again,
The elves are breaking into zen.
With marshmallow wars on every street,
And cookies vanished—what a feat!

Neighbors have lights that blink and glow,
But one house shines a strange purple show.
They claim it's art, but who can tell?
It looks more like a giant bell.

A snow globe filled with snowball fights,
As cousins argue about the rights.
We all agree, 'tis the season,
For laughter's our only reason!

# A Tapestry of Holiday Cheer

Wreaths made from soggy old bread,
At Christmas brunch, we laugh instead.
A feast of dreams, a pie that's burnt,
Yet sweetened spirits never hurt.

Elves on skates in disco lights,
Dance around like silly sights.
A llama wearing festive bows,
With cookies stashed within his toes.

Mistletoe hanging from the door,
Aunt Gen's still trying to score more.
With every hug, a squeaky toy,
We celebrate with goofy joy.

Presents wrapped in newspaper scrap,
Hidden well, oh what a trap!
As laughter fills the jolly air,
We find that love is everywhere.

## **Snowflakes in a Rainbow Dance**

Snowflakes twirl like ballerinas,
Each one says, 'Look, I'm a diva!'
While kids build forts from winter's gems,
With snowball fights as silly diadems.

Sledding down a rainbow hill,
With laughter loud, our hearts do fill.
One falls down, a tumble and roll,
We cheer them on—what a goal!

The hot cocoa, thick as stew,
I dropped my marshmallows, how about you?
Gifts exchanged with silly names,
Like 'Best Sleepyhead' and 'King of Games.'

Twinkling lights in every hue,
Each bulb a story, old and new.
In this merry, vibrant trance,
We join the snowflakes in their dance.

## **Heartfelt Reflections**

In December's grip, we bake and we cheer,
Mistakes with the cookies—watch out for the deer!
The lights on the tree, tangled like my hair,
Grandma's wild tales, does anyone really care?

Snowmen in gardens, with noses so bright,
They look like they're judging, is that just the light?
I trip on the tinsel, it's stuck to my shoe,
The cat's in the tree—what else is new?

Uncles are snoring, and kids start to spin,
Fights over the last piece of holiday din.
Mixed drinks are flowing, who's counting the cups?
I'm ready for naps, but the party erupts!

With laughter and chaos, the days slip away,
Memories made, come what may, come what may.
In this festive madness, joy's hard to find,
Yet each laugh and mishap, is one of a kind.

## **Kaleidoscope of Year-End Reflections**

Elves in the corner, with coffee to sip,
Plotting in whispers, as I take a trip.
The fruitcake is here, it's oddly shaped too,
Like my cousin's dance moves, they confuse and skew!

Wrapping with paper, oh what a delight,
Scissors and ribbons scattered left and right.
I'm losing my marbles, it's all a big blur,
If I can just find the gift for Auntie Fleur!

Snowflakes are falling, like confetti from dreams,
The reindeer are tipsy, or so so it seems.
Pine needles stick like confessions in jest,
Under the mistletoe, strange lips feel blessed!

As the year takes a bow and begins to unwind,
We cherish the laughter, the fun intertwined.
Raise a glass full of cheer for our silly parade,
With friends and with family, let joy cascade!

## Echoes of Laughter Beneath the Stars

In a cozy cabin, with lights so bright,
We gather 'round, oh what a sight!
With cookies flying and laughter loud,
We're the silliest bunch, so proud.

A reindeer costume? Oh, what a joke!
Fetching eggnog while trying not to choke.
With whispers of secrets in frosty air,
We giggle like children without a care.

Tinsel tangled in Auntie's hair,
Is it a decoration or just despair?
We dance to tunes from a distant age,
As Grandma twirls like a festive sage.

Underneath the stars, a chorus sings,
Harmonizing with the joy that this night brings.
With echoes of laughter that fill the night,
We gather together, hearts so light.

## **Colorful Crystals on a Winter Night**

The snowflakes twirl, a dazzling show,
But watch out, they'll land on your nose, you know!
As we build snowmen, we can't resist,
A carrot or two for a snowman's kiss.

With scarves wrapped tight and mittens too,
Oh look! There's a penguin—wait, that's Cousin Drew!
This winter wonderland, what a delight,
With colorful crystals that shine in the night.

Hot cocoa spills as we take a sip,
Chocolate on faces, a merry trip.
We wear fluffiest sweaters, bright and bold,
Trading stories of warmth through the bitter cold.

In the moon's glow, we make snow angels wide,
But it seems we've lost track of the snowy slide.
So here's to the giggles that fill the air,
Colorful moments, too silly to compare.

## A Wreath of Wishes

A wreath hangs crooked, but who really cares?
It's got ribbons and bows, and last year's repairs.
With wishes attached and dreams on display,
We laugh about all the plans gone astray.

The neighbors peek in, their eyes open wide,
As we wrestle with decorations that bicker and slide.
Lights twinkle on trees, with strands gone askew,
It's a festive fun house, our laughter's the glue.

We hang up the stockings, all four on one hook,
A few look like socks, well, that was the hook!
Silly surprises will come when we wake,
Like socks that are stuffed with sweet cakes to bake.

A wreath of wishes, oh, what a scene,
With glitter and dreams that simply can't be seen.
In this joyful chaos, we raise up a toast,
To funny memories, we cherish the most.

## **Footprints in the Frost**

Footprints in frost, a path to delight,
Whose big snow boots left this mess overnight?
We giggle and snicker as we stomp through the snow,
Tracing our steps in a flurry-like show.

Snowball fights break out, a wild, crazy spree,
One hit Grandma, but oh, it was me!
With laughter erupting and squeals in the air,
We build a fierce fort, too big to compare.

The puppy joins in, with leaps and a bound,
Chasing his tail to the merry sound.
With noses red and cheeks all aglow,
We sip steaming cider, just like a pro.

Footprints in frost tell the tales of our fun,
As we make all the memories until the day's done.
With cheer all around, there's a warmth in our hearts,
These moments of joy are truly fine arts.

## The Palette of December

The red of reindeer noses, bright,
Goes well with green tights, what a sight!
With snowflakes dancing all around,
And auntie's fruitcake hitting the ground.

We hang our socks, both big and small,
One for the cat, who's bound to sneak and sprawl.
Eggnog spills on the holiday cheer,
As Uncle Joe begins to shout, 'I'm here!'

Pine trees twinkle with lights galore,
While family debates, 'Who brought the floor?'
Grandma's knitting, but dropped a stitch,
Just as Uncle Ted becomes quite the witch.

Wrapping paper's a sticky mess,
Covered in glitter, we can't impress.
With laughter echoing, we all partake,
In this colorful chaos, for goodness' sake!

**Scented Pine and Sugar Plums**

Sugar plums dancing in our heads,
While grandpa snores in his cozy bed.
Pine needles sneak underfoot in style,
As we tiptoe by, hoping for a smile.

The cookies are burnt, or so I hear,
The frosting's a mix of laughter and cheer.
Mom's in the kitchen, a flurry of fun,
While we argue if the eggnog's too run.

Card games bring on a curious fate,
As Aunt Sue claims she just won the plate.
Uncle Mike's belt won't hold after pie,
But he insists it's the cookies that fly.

As snowflakes jingle, we all agree,
December's blend of joy, just like a spree.
So here's to the mishaps, the laughs, and the love,
As we tuck them away, like gifts from above!

## Starlit Paths Through Snow

Starlight twinkles on a frozen lake,
As ice skaters slip, oh, what a break!
With rosy cheeks and laughter to share,
Someone's mittens end up in midair!

Sledding down hills with a glorious yell,
While Grandma is brewing her famous swell.
Snowmen stand guard with curious stares,
One's wearing a hat made of old underwear!

The merry tunes of carols float high,
As we all sing mixed up, oh me, oh my!
The dog in the snow made a bundle of bliss,
Chasing after snowflakes, he leaps with a kiss.

Underneath the stars, we glow in delight,
With food fights and snowballs through the night.
In this season of goofiness, we take flight,
As the world wraps us up in soft winter light.

## Mirth of the Midwinter Moon

Beneath the moon, so shiny and bright,
We gather around, sharing tales of the night.
The hot cocoa's questionable, with odd bits,
While Grandpa insists it's the marshmallow hits.

Mittens are lost, like socks in the wash,
And snowflakes fall down in a furious nosh.
With snowball fights turning into a race,
The neighbor thinks chaos has won first place!

The laughter exudes from every cold breath,
While Auntie shows off her epic new meth.
We cheer her on with a wink and a nod,
In this wintery madness, we're happily flawed.

As twinkling lights beckon, we shout with glee,
In this madcap moment, we're wild and free.
So here's to the memories woven with glee,
In the mirth of the moon, just you wait and see!

## Cards and Candles and Cheer

In a box of cards, a treasure lies,
Old names scribbled, oh what a surprise!
From Auntie Sue to cousin Fred,
And memories dance in my festive head.

The candles flicker, some a bit bent,
The wax drips low, like money well spent.
We light them up for a laugh and a cheer,
Watch them wobble, oh what a fear!

Glitter spills like a snowstorm bright,
On a card that promises everyone's alright.
I'll send them out, with a grin and a joke,
Pray they don't end up as a weird family poke.

Oh joy and laughter, all wrapped in a bow,
As I sip my cider, feeling the glow.
With cards and candles to set the stage,
This holiday season, I'll act my age!

## **Old Carols and New Memories**

We gather 'round for the songs of yore,
Off-key renditions make us laugh more.
That jolly tune of the winter's delight,
With no clue of words, we sing through the night.

Carolers shriek with all their might,
While the neighbors just shake their heads in fright.
They came for cheer, but what they got,
Is a concert that's best, just not taught.

Memories made in our festive abode,
As we sip hot cocoa and laugh at the load.
The melodies twist, the voices collide,
It's a merry disaster, and we can't hide.

So here's to the old and the new that we make,
To laughter and love, for goodness' sake.
A chorus of chaos, a joyful delight,
This holiday spirit, we embrace with all our might!

## **Ribbons of Remembrance**

Ribbons scattered, all over the floor,
Gift wrapping chaos, oh what a chore!
Colors bright, and patterns that clash,
Like last year's dance moves, a hilarious bash.

I find the leftover rolls, half-used in vain,
Wrap up my gift with a sly little gain.
That bow on top? A masterpiece! (Not)
Tied like my shoelaces — oh, so distraught!

Each ribbon tells tales from celebrations past,
Of awkward family photos that never held fast.
Grandpa's big grin and Aunt Meg's wild hair,
In every twist, a laugh — oh, I swear!

So let's tie these memories with laughter and cheer,
With ribbons of fun, let's share a good sneer.
For the holidays come, with joy in their wake,
And who can resist a good chuckle? For goodness sake!

## The Magic of Mistletoe

Under the sprigs of this leafy affair,
I stand with my crush, oh what a scare!
Do you kiss? Or just grimace and frown?
The awkwardness wraps me like a bright gown.

Each year it hangs with a twinkle and glee,
But all I can think is, 'What's wrong with me?'
My pals all dare me with a mischievous grin,
And I ponder my fate — awkwardness win!

So there we go, a peck on the cheek,
With a hapless smile, and my heart makes a squeak.
Jingle bells echo, as I walk away fast,
Still wondering how long this moment will last.

The magic of moments, oh what a trick,
Turning sweet thoughts into a comedy flick.
With laughter and blush, the season's delight,
Every kiss under mistletoe feels just right!

# Ornamented Pastels of the Heart

Candy canes in every hue,
Twinkle lights shining bright too.
Socks that rival a clown's attire,
Who knew that joy could catch on fire?

Pudding that jiggles, makes me laugh,
Lights that dangle, a dazzling gaff.
Mittens mismatched, what a delight,
Let's wear them all, it feels so right!

Tinsel falling like a snow,
Each shiny thread a silly show.
Laughter bubbles, what a feat,
A holiday here that can't be beat!

With colors mixed, and giggles loud,
In this season, I feel so proud.
Not just red, nor just pearl white,
Festive cheer is our birthright!

## The Glow of Hope and Unity

Toasting marshmallows with a flair,
S'mores that stick to every chair.
Snowmen wobbling, can they stand?
Here's where fun's got the upper hand!

Mistletoe hangs, but who will dare?
To kiss a friend with wild hair!
Gifts that rattle and sometimes squeak,
Unwrapping chaos—oh, what a peek!

Eggnog spills on grandma's dress,
Oops! There goes the Christmas press.
Frogs in sweaters jump with glee,
Who knew a tree could be that free?

Candles dancing like they know,
Their waxen legs put on quite a show.
Unity's glow, it sparkles bright,
Through silly times, we find our light!

## A Rainbow of Comfort in Chilly Air

Scarves that tie like pretzel knots,
Hot cocoa flows in jolly pots.
Snowflakes falling, each unique,
A world so wacky, not for the weak!

Pine needles tickle, oh so merry,
While fruitcake sits, a food cemetery.
The partridge sings from its faux tree,
Do parrots really wish to be free?

With mittens lost, we brave the chill,
A frosty bite gives quite a thrill.
Bubbling laughter fills the night,
In this odd winter, all feels right!

Chili cook-offs that go astray,
Colors swirling in a comical fray.
Under the moon, we dance and sway,
Despite the cold, let's laugh away!

## **Seasonal Stories in Every Shade**

Belly laughs around the feast,
A turkey chase, oh what a beast!
Pin the nose on Rudolph's face,
These quirky games, we keep the pace!

Wrapping paper fights ensue,
Bows that fly like little birds too.
A sleigh ride that's just a wild game,
In every tale, we're never the same!

From mittens lost to trees askew,
Our memories blend like a vibrant brew.
Funny stories that never end,
In every heart, we find a friend!

Colored lights that make us grin,
With joy and laughter layered within.
In every shade, let joy entwine,
For the spirit here is totally divine!

## Hallowed Hues of Enchantment

Twinkling lights dance on the tree,
A squirrel steals ornaments with glee.
Santa's stuck in the chimney, oh dear,
While reindeer laugh, bringing festive cheer.

Mismatched socks and odd hats,
Grandma's baking the world's worst spats.
Elves on break, sipping hot cocoa,
While snowmen plot a frosty combo.

Laughter echoes as gifts unite,
Wrapping fails that are quite the sight.
A wreath upside down, what a thrill,
Guess it's time for another refill!

With every blooper, joy's out to play,
We cherish our mishaps, come what may.
So raise a mug, let stories unfold,
In every hue, our laughter is gold.

## Nature's Colors in the Festival of Lights

Evergreen trees, not straight but grand,
Covered in glitter dust from a hand.
The cat in tinsel, quite the purr,
A fashion statement, oh what a blur!

Snowflakes expecting to dance in lines,
But here they fall, creating funny signs.
Kids make angels, but one heads south,
Now there's a snowman with a carrot mouth!

The cookies are burnt, but who even cares?
Taste-testing always leads to funny glares.
Wrapping paper stuck on a shoe,
Each sticky step leads to much ado.

With every moment wrapped in delight,
We gather 'round in our colorful light.
Nature's chaos is a wondrous spree,
As we celebrate with glee and glee!

## A Prism of Memories and Dreams

Memories glow like lights on the wall,
While Uncle Joe tells tales that enthrall.
From a bowtie mishap to fruitcake fights,
We laugh until we share our delights.

Mom's holiday dress looks like a tree,
A prism of colors, now that's the key!
Our family table, a feast of odd,
From jellied salads to potatoes, a fraud.

Oh, look at Frank, caught in the lights,
He's now a disco ball, a sight that excites!
With every chuckle, our spirits soar high,
As snowflakes fall gently from the sky.

Cherished moments, a grand jumbled brew,
Each laugh and each joke, a sweet kind of glue.
In this chaos, our hearts truly gleam,
A prism of joy in every shared dream.

## Carving Joy with Every Brushstroke

Painting the porch with colors so bright,
A stroke of disaster, a comical sight.
Gingerbread houses leaning to the side,
Each sagging roof filled with holiday pride.

Decking the halls goes hilariously wrong,
Drapes turning drapes into a 'Whoops!' song.
With mismatched baubles, we create our flair,
This festive chaos, beyond compare!

Frosty the snowman can't quite stand tall,
Yet he wobbles around, giving it his all.
With paintbrush in hand, we create our zone,
In every mishap, we find our own home.

So here's to the laughter, that fills up the air,
Creating joy, with love everywhere.
In every stroke, a giggle awaits,
As we celebrate fun that life creates!

## **Nights Draped in Starlight**

Beneath the lights we share a laugh,
A cat in a hat, our biggest gaffe.
Snowflakes dance, we slip and slide,
Chasing joy like a runaway ride.

With cocoa spills and marshmallows high,
A squirrel steals cookies, oh my, oh my!
Laughter bubbles like a fizzy drink,
In all the chaos, we play and wink.

Dancing shadows, twinkling bright,
We sing off-key in the frosty night.
Every whisper turns into a jest,
Making memories, that's our quest.

So raise a toast to our silly fights,
On this jolly eve, with starlit sights.
Through quirks and blunders, here we stay,
Wrapped in laughter, night and day.

## Family Ties Across Time

Gather 'round the table tight,
Uncle Fred's jokes, a constant fright.
Grandma's pie, a sight to behold,
But please, don't eat it; it's moldy and old!

Auntie Sue's stories, oh what a bore,
Of her cat's birthday—wasn't it four?
We roll our eyes, yet grin with glee,
Her tales, like fine wine—just let them be.

The kids with crayons, a colorful spree,
Painting each other as Santa and tree.
With giggles erupting from each little face,
We find goofy joy in our silly place.

So raise your glass to the quirks we know,
In this family circus, where love will grow.
Through laughter and chaos, we shine so bright,
Together we stand, our hearts alight.

**Diversions in the Frost**

Outside the snowflakes tumble and glide,
Time for a snowball fight, let's not hide!
The dog joins in, with a bark and a leap,
As we tumble and roll in a snowdrift heap.

With sleds and laughter, we race down the hill,
Coffees forgotten—it's all a thrill!
Face-red from laughing, we bundle and hug,
While sipping hot cocoa, just an old mug.

A snowman with broomstick stands over there,
With a carrot nose, and quite the flair.
But wait, it seems he's lost his hat,
Now we're on a quest—imagine that!

The cold may bite, but hearts are warm,
In playful madness, we weather the storm.
Let's dance in the snow, with frosty cheer,
In these silly moments, joy draws near.

## **Memories Wrapped in Ribbons**

Every gift topped with a bow so grand,
Yet what's inside? A mystery planned!
Last year's sock got mixed in the fun,
Is it a gift, or a prank well done?

Uncle Joe's ties are a colorful sight,
With stripes and dots, a dazzling fright.
We gather 'round to see who unwraps,
With squeals of laughter, no need for maps.

Grandpa's old sweater, a treasure today,
Fashionably awful, in a kitschy way.
"Wear it with pride!" he winks with a grin,
In our goofy fashion show, it's sure to win.

As ribbons fall and papers fly,
Ambassadors of joy, reaching the sky.
In every chuckle, in each silly gift,
We weave our memories, the spirits lift.

## **The Colors of Warmth and Wonder**

Twinkling lights in every hue,
A purple Santa? Yes, that's new!
Eggnog flows like silly dreams,
While snowmen plot in wacky schemes.

Garlands hang from every door,
A cat climbs high, then falls to the floor!
Red and green, a festive fight,
As mom's burnt cookies spark delight.

Socks lined with candy, oh what a sight!
A mix-up leads to a laugh tonight.
With laughter shared and hugs exchanged,
In this season, joy's unchained!

From silly hats to dancing fools,
We'll roast marshmallows, break all the rules!
A rainbow wonder, oh what fun,
In this warmth, we've surely won!

## Radiant Reflections of the Season

The tree is dressed in tinsel bright,
With ornaments that cause a fright!
Granddad's sweater, a sight to see,
Looks like a beast from a holiday spree.

Pine-scented candles flicker and sway,
While unwrapping gifts goes hilariously astray.
A gag gift joke, a rubber chicken,
In this madness, laughter's the mission.

Cookies for Santa, but wait there's more,
An olive, a pickle, and candy galore!
Presents piled high, a jungle to roam,
You never know when pets call it home.

As carols echo through the night,
Choir of kids who are far too bright,
Melodies that make no earthly sense,
A cacophony of festive pretense!

## Echoes of Merry Melodies

Jingle bells collide with silly songs,
A choir of dogs joins in along!
Carrying tunes both loud and weird,
While neighbors squint, yet cheered and cheered.

Presents wrapped in paper gone wrong,
Tangled ribbons, a slapstick throng!
Confetti falls like snow from above,
And all around, it's pure holiday love.

Jolly laughter fills the air,
As Grandma shows off her dance flair.
With slippers sliding 'cross the floor,
We'll all join in for just one more!

Tinsel tossed in chaotic grace,
Reflects the joy on every face.
This jolly time, we sing along,
In a world where silliness belongs!

## The Glistening Canvas of December

Snowflakes fall like glitter bombs,
Painting landscapes, nature's charms.
Yet somehow through the white and gray,
A rainbow scarf leads us astray.

Cookies dressed in frosting bling,
What's this? A cake that's doing the swing?
Sprinkle fights turn cheeks to glee,
Sweet chaos, oh how merry we'll be!

Ornaments dancing on tree boughs high,
As little ones gaze up with a sigh.
Magical moments feasting with cheer,
A feast for fools who hold fun dear.

With laughter ringing 'round the fire,
Stories shared that never tire.
As the night crafts its chilly embrace,
Every heart finds a warm, bright place!

## A Canvas of Frost and Cheer

Snowflakes dance on roofs so bold,
While hot cocoa dreams unfold.
Gifts wrapped in ribbons, oh so bright,
Elves in pajamas, what a sight!

Tinsel tangled, lights gone wild,
A cat in a tree, Christmas styled.
A snowman with a carrot nose,
Wears my old socks, I suppose!

Warm mittens lost, another quest,
My kid wearing two mismatched vests!
Jingle bells and laughter soar,
Who misplaced the cookies? Oh, what a chore!

With frosty breath we race outside,
On sleds that hold our awkward pride.
A canvas painted with cheerful glee,
In this wacky winter jubilee!

## Harmonies in Holly

Carols sung off-key and loud,
A chorus of laughter draws a crowd.
Mistletoe hangs, time to take chance,
With a twirl and a goofy dance!

Grandma's fruitcake? No one will bite,
Yet it shines like a Christmas light.
Neighbors argue whose lights must blink,
While kids in the corner quietly drink!

Wrapping paper flying, not a shred,
Uncle Joe's asleep, resting his head.
Christmas trees, with ornaments askew,
Yet it's a masterpiece—who knew?

Hot soup spills on Dad's best tie,
While cousins giggle and shout, oh my!
With harmonies sweet and mischief in mind,
This holiday spirit is one of a kind!

## **Cherished Moments by Candlelight**

Candle flickers, shadows jump,
Uncle Sam just gave a loud thump.
Grandma's stories flying around,
As we all settle on the ground!

Board games stacked, a mountain tall,
One wrong move, watch them all fall!
With laughter echoing through the night,
And a giant Santa brought to light!

Sweets piled high, oh what a treat,
Chocolate fudge and cookies to eat.
The dog snags a gingerbread man,
Chaos spreads with just one plan!

Photos snapped, goofy grins bright,
Mismatched hats in festive light.
Mom's hat's too big, Dad's too tight,
But these cherished moments feel just right!

## **Frosty Breath and Warm Hearts**

Frosty breath whispers in the air,
While waiters juggle, unaware.
A snowball fight goes out of hand,
Like an epic battle planned!

Hot drinks spill, laughter erupts,
But who would have thought, oh, what's up?
With fuzzy socks and slippers worn,
We dance around, our spirits born!

Gifts exchanged with a wink and grin,
As Aunt Betty makes her entrance spin.
The tree leans, but never fears,
For it holds our love, among the cheers!

With frosty breath, we raise a toast,
To funny moments we love the most.
Warm hearts glow with joy we share,
Our holiday is beyond compare!

## Cedars and Candy Canes

In winter's grasp, the trees get dressed,
With ornaments hanging, they look their best.
But one cheeky squirrel, on a sugar spree,
Nibbled the garland, just wait and see.

The lights twinkled bright on the house next door,
But his acorn stash made him start to snore.
He woke with a jolt, all covered in snow,
Mistaken for Santa, a jolly old pro!

The cat climbed the tree, with a leap and a flair,
Tangled in tinsel, oh what a scare!
With laughter erupting, the family reigned,
This Christmas chaos was joyfully gained.

So raise up a glass, to the season's delight,
Where candy canes sparkle in the moonlight.
Let the laughter echo, and fun never cease,
In this merry madness, we find our peace.

## **Nestled Dreams in the Snow**

Snowflakes are falling, a white fluffy bed,
The kids build a snowman, with a carrot for head.
But it seems he has dreams of a tropical spot,
Wishing for warmth, oh why not a yacht?

With marshmallow clouds on a cocoa throne,
Imagining beaches while wrapped in flannel,
We laugh at his whims, what a silly thing,
A snowman in sunglasses, planning to swing!

Each flurry of laughter, like snowflakes that twirl,
Spinning in joy, what a whimsical world.
So let's share a giggle, and warmth from within,
As dreams of hot summers swirl 'round like a grin.

And when night descends, with stars shining bright,
We'll cuddle up close, to chase off the night.
In this frosty fun, so cozy and sweet,
The dreams that we build make the season complete.

## A Season of Giving Back

Tinsel and troubles, oh what a sight,
The gifts pile up, such a curious height.
But Aunt Edna's fruitcake, tucked in with glee,
Is a challenge for even the bravest of me!

The children are bouncing, all filled with cheer,
While the cat is plotting to shred wrapping near.
With laughter exploding, it's hard to resist,
Who knew that holiday bliss came with a twist?

As carols ring out, and the cocoa flows,
We stumble on gifts wrapped in mismatched bows.
A sock stuffed with candy, a hat for the dog,
Still makes it a party, not even a fog!

So let's raise our mugs, with giggles and glee,
It's not just the gifts, but the fun that we see.
In the spirit of giving, we find simple tracks,
This season we're all in, and we're giving back!

## **Unconventional Traditions**

Grandpa's in charge of the family feast,
But his cooking skills? Well, to say the least...
He throws in some pickles, a splash of hot sauce,
Declared it a winner, but it's quite the loss!

A cat in a sweater, with glitter and flair,
The dog steals the show, oh what a wild pair!
They sit 'neath the table, looking for scraps,
As we share our stories and laughter erupts like a clap.

Mom's secret recipe is lost in the haze,
She's made it with cupcakes, it's just a phase.
With frosting for snow and gumdrops on top,
Who knew that for dessert, we'd all take a flop?

So let's toast to the moments that make our hearts glow,
With traditions so silly, they steal the show.
In all of this laughter, our hearts take flight,
Who needs perfection, when it's all just so bright?

**Fireside Stories and Family Bonds**

Cousins wrestling by the tree,
Mom's secret stash, we all agree.
Uncle Dave's tales never quite right,
Laughter echoes deep into the night.

Socks hung low, a cat at play,
Mistletoe? Well, what can I say!
Grandma's cookies, a perfect flop,
Yet in our hearts, we'll never stop.

## **Whimsical Whispers of Wonder**

Elves in pajamas, a curious sight,
Santa's reindeer lost in flight.
Pine cones glimmer, they giggle and sway,
While kids plot gifts they'll give away.

Rudolph's nose, oh, what a glow,
Mom said, 'Put it down, it's not a show!'
Tinsel tangled in our hair,
This festive madness, none can compare!

**The Festive Embroidery of Life**

Stitching memories with every cheer,
A snowman's hat? Still missing this year!
Frosty windows with stories to tell,
As we trip over each other in the shell.

Gifts wrapped boldly, but late for sure,
A paper avalanche, a playful lure.
Mom's classic fruitcake, a fearsome bite,
With every slice, we dodge for our life!

## Pages from the Book of December

Reading tales of cheer and glee,
Dad lost in dreams beneath the tree.
Ratscheting laughter fills the air,
While Grandma hides the chocolate fare.

A gingerbread hat! Oh, what a feat,
The family dog? He's eyeing a treat.
Slipping on wrapping, we tumble and roll,
As holiday spirit steals the show!

## The Symphony of Cocoa and Cinnamon

In mugs so large, hot fizzy brew,
With marshmallow fluff, a sweet debut.
Whisking up giggles with every swoosh,
As chocolate rivers start to woosh!

A sprinkle of joy in every sip,
Slurping away, such a merry trip.
The cat steals a spoon, oh what a sight,
While cocoa mustache greets the night!

Churro churps as the cookies dance,
Whirling on plates, oh what a prance!
Tummies rumbling, we share a feast,
Cocoa confessions, laughter's the least!

With every sip, our worries flee,
In this hot brew, we all agree.
The laughter and joy, oh what a score,
Here's to cocoa—who could ask for more?

## Candlelight and Crimson Wishes

A flicker here, a shimmer there,
Candles wobble, wax everywhere!
With crimson ribbons tied so tight,
The tree's a sight, oh what a fright!

Pine needles dance to a clumsy beat,
As grandma's cookies claim the seat.
Sparkling lights, they're twirling round,
I swear they're plotting, so profound!

Each present wrapped with love and cheer,
Only to find out, it's full of sheer!
Billy's socks! Oh what a joke,
Holiday giggles from each poke!

Mismatched bows, a playful twist,
When gifts are opened, they can't be missed.
With every laugh, we take a vow,
Crimson wishes light our brow!

## **Vibrant Whispers of Silent Nights**

Silent night? Oh, what a sham!
They're singing loudly, the chaos jam!
From carolers bold to pets that howl,
It's a nighttime circus, hear their growl!

Snowflakes tumble like a wild dance,
Falling fast in a snowy trance.
Scarfed-up snowmen, they pose for photos,
But their eyes are frosty—oh, what a woe!

As kids throw snowballs, they hit the mark,
Though uncle just fell in the park!
Laughter erupts as the fun takes flight,
Vibrant whispers fill the night!

A snowman's top hat takes off on its own,
Cackling laughter fills up the zone.
With warmth in our hearts and spirits so bright,
We share the joy of these vibrant nights!

## The Wonderland of Warm-Hearted Gatherings

Gather round for a jolly feast,
Grandma's secrets for supper, at least!
Cousins poke fun and sisters will tease,
With plates piled high, let's eat with ease!

The dog sneaks bites, oh what a shame,
While he glances around, playing the game.
Forks in the air, it's a food fight,
Oh what a scene, what a merry sight!

Crafters creating bizarre decor,
With glittering wishes, who could ask for more?
From seeds for laughter, we proudly sow,
This warmth of gathering helps us grow!

In this wondrous place, we spread delight,
With hugs and giggles igniting the night.
Let's cherish these moments, our hearts will sing,
In a wonderland that joy will bring!

Milton Keynes UK
Ingram Content Group UK Ltd.
UKHW021927011224
451790UK00005B/49

9 789916 908389